Problem Solving KS1

Pete Hall

HOPSCOTCH
EDUCATIONAL PUBLISHING

Published by
Hopscotch Educational Publishing Ltd,
29 Waterloo Place,
Leamington Spa CV32 5LA
Tel: 01926 744227

© 2002 Hopscotch Educational Publishing

Written by Pete Hall
Series design by Blade Communications
Cover illustration by Susan Hutchison
Illustrated by Susan Hutchison
Printed by Clintplan

ISBN 1-902239-99-7

Problem Solving KS1

'The ability to solve problems is at the heart of mathematics.'

Mathematics Counts 1982

Problem solving has always been an important but neglected element of mathematics. Far too much of mathematics teaching concentrated on the practice and consolidation of number skills in isolation from the broader context, ie why we needed to learn the skills. The introduction of the National Curriculum for mathematics, with its emphasis on 'Using and applying' was a forward step. However since the launch of the National Numeracy Strategy and the *Framework for Teaching Mathematics* there appears to have been a decline in the emphasis on problem solving. Indeed the HMI Evaluation of the National Numeracy Strategy (2001) reports that, 'in the main teaching activity, problem solving is still underemphasised'.

This book offers 18 problem-solving lessons. Each lesson combines teaching objectives from the Solving problems section of the *Framework for Teaching Mathematics* with objectives from the general sections. This approach will provide more time within the mathematics curriculum because objectives are combined and linked. Each lesson is aimed at providing children with a challenging learning experience with the emphasis on enjoyment. Mathematics is a wonderfully exciting and rewarding subject and it is vital as teachers that we communicate this to our children.

Problem solving qualities

In order to make progress in problem-solving activities children need to develop a range of skills or qualities that are not specific to mathematics. Many children can find problem solving very daunting because they have not developed these necessary qualities. Therefore it is vital that schools start to develop them in Key Stage 1 and continue to develop them throughout the children's school careers. Schools should discuss how they could develop these necessary qualities, which include the following.

- The ability to discuss, work cooperatively and work individually.
- The ability to communicate using mathematics.
- The ability to define and understand problems.

- The ability to think of key questions.
- The ability to explore and experiment.
- The ability to recognise 'blind alleys'.
- The ability to develop 'transfer skills'.
- The ability to use imagination and flexibility of mind.
- The ability to be reflective.
- The ability to persevere.

Mathematical problem solving skills

In addition to the generic qualities listed above, the National Curriculum lists these skills.

Using and applying number

Pupils should be taught to:

Problem solving

a) Approach problems involving number, and data presented in a variety of forms, in order to identify what they need to do.
b) Develop flexible approaches to problem solving and look for ways to overcome difficulties.
c) Make decisions about which operations and problem-solving strategies to use.
d) Organise and check their work.

Communicating

e) Use the correct language, symbols and vocabulary associated with number and data.
f) Communicate in spoken, pictorial and written form, at first using informal language and recording, then mathematical language and symbols.

Reasoning

g) Present results in an organised way.
h) Understand a general statement and investigate whether particular cases match it.
i) Explain their methods and reasoning when solving problems involving number and data.

The lessons

Each lesson follows the same format.

Learning objectives
These are taken directly from the Yearly teaching programmes in the *Framework for Teaching Mathematics*. The solving problems objectives are linked with at least one other objective.

Vocabulary
This lists all the appropriate words and phrases to be used in the lesson. It is vital that children should see these words as well as hear them. So they should either be written on the board or if sets of vocabulary cards are available use these.

Resources
The lessons have been written to use a minimum of resources. Most of the resources listed would be found in most primary classrooms. Some lessons have resource sheets or activity sheets that can be photocopied.

Oral and mental starter
These short sessions are intended to provide the children with a lively and fun start to the lesson. The objectives are taken from the National Numeracy Strategy's sample medium-term planning.

Teaching points
A detailed lesson plan to guide you through the lesson. The emphasis is on lively activities that will demonstrate to the children that mathematics is alive!

Plenary
All the plenaries have been planned to allow the children to reflect on what has gone before. Often there are 'challenges' included in the plenary. The principle here is to ensure that the children's ability is challenged but in a non-threatening way.

Support and Extension
These sections are aimed to support the less able and challenge the more able. The nature of problem solving is such that much of the work is 'open ended' and therefore differentiation should be more manageable.

Questions to guide assessment
Teacher assessment is an important component of teaching. These questions are included to help you focus on a small number of issues. The nature of problem solving is such that it is very difficult to make summative judgements. For example, 'Presents results in an organised way'. The child in Reception can do this in one way and a Y6 child in another way but both could be as valid. It is up to teachers to use their professional judgement through teacher assessment.

Calculators

Some of the lessons involve the use of calculators and in particular the OHP calculator. This is a very powerful learning tool for young children.

Wherever the calculator is suggested it is used to support children's learning. Therefore the approach in these books is in line with the recommendations of the National Numeracy Strategy.

How many ways?

Framework for Numeracy objectives

Solving problems: Reasoning about numbers or shapes
○ Solve simple problems or puzzles in a practical context, and respond to 'What could we try next?'

Counting and recognising numbers
○ Count reliably up to 10 everyday objects.

Measures, shape and space
○ Use everyday words to describe position.

VOCABULARY

above, below, bottom, check, count, cube, different, how many ? side, square, ten, top, put together

Resources
○ Cubes
○ Photocopiable Sheets 1 to 4 (pages 42 to 45)
○ Blu-tack
○ Number lines

Oral and mental starter

Objective: Count reliably up to 10 objects

○ The oral and mental starter is included in the main part of the lesson.

Problem-solving challenge

> *How many different ways can 10 cubes be arranged on squared paper?*

With the whole class

○ Explain to the children that today's challenge is to try and find as many ways as they can of putting 10 cubes on to squared paper to make shapes. Demonstrate this by asking a child to count out 10 cubes at the front of the class. Ask the rest of the children to count aloud in unison.

○ Stop the children at certain points and ask questions such as:

   'What number comes next?'

   'What number is 2 more than where we are now?'

○ Ask the child holding the cubes to cover them up. Ask questions like:

   'How many cubes are hidden?'

   'If I take 1 cube away how many cubes will I have then?'

○ When 10 cubes are counted out, select a few children to put Blu-tack on them. Demonstrate how to fix them on the large squared paper. The rule is that the cubes have to be placed together exactly side by side.

 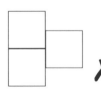

Ask the children to count the cubes as you point to them.

○ Invite a couple of children to come out and arrange the cubes in different ways. Ask:

   'Are you going to put them all in a straight line?'

   'Are you going to make a shape with them?'

Children working in pairs

- Tell the children that they have to work in pairs to find as many different ways as they can to arrange the 10 cubes on the squared paper. Give them copies of photocopiable Sheet 1 (page 42) and ask them to draw coloured dots on the squared paper to show where the cubes went. Then ask them to draw a coloured line around the complete shape that they made with their cubes. Encourage them to invent names for their shapes!

- Tell them that, to make sure the rest of the cubes don't feel lonely, they have to use a different 10 cubes for each shape! This will give them plenty of practice in counting. Ask:

  'How can you check that you have got 10 cubes?'

- It is good practice for children to get into the habit of checking. Ask:

  'How many different ways could there be of arranging the 10 cubes?'

- Go around the class to ensure that the children understand the activity and are doing it correctly.

- When they have found enough ways, give them either Sheet 2, 3 or 4 (pages 43 to 45), according to their level of achievement. Tell them to count the number of cubes in each shape on the sheet and write the answer next to the shape.

- The activity sheets will act as a guide to assessing the children's ability to count to 10 and beyond.

Plenary

- Choose some children to show their sheets. Ask questions such as:

  'How many shapes did you get?'

  'What did you call them?'

  'Has anyone got any more?'

  'How did you check that you had got 10 cubes each time?'

  'Did anyone else check in a different way?'

- Talk about the shapes using correct language such as 'long', 'wide' and 'symmetrical'. Explain the meaning of these words as you go along.

- Establish that there are lots of ways to arrange the 10 cubes. Ask:

  'Did you always count in ones?'

  'Are there other ways you can count them?'

  The idea is that the children begin to use different strategies to count, such as in twos. Some might recognise that a square shape of four cubes will always be four cubes, so they can put four in their heads and count on.

Support

- Limit the number of cubes to a number that the children can comfortably count up to. They should then be able to join in with the same activity as the rest of the class.

- Write the following letters on the board: L E I H T. Ask the children how many cubes they would use to make shape L on squared paper. They can repeat this with the other letters.

- These children should do photocopiable Sheet 2.

Extension

- Use as many cubes as the ability of the children allows.

- Let the children use as many cubes as they want and set the challenge of finding as many square shapes as they can with their cubes.

- These children should do photocopiable Sheet 4.

Questions to guide assessment

- How did the children count the cubes?
- Did they count accurately?
- Did they check their counting and, if so, how?
- Did any of the children use a simple strategy to try to solve the challenge?

How many wellies?

Framework for Numeracy objectives

Solving problems: Problems involving 'real life'

○ Use developing mathematical ideas and methods to solve practical problems involving counting and comparing in a real context.

Counting and recognising numbers

○ Count reliably up to 10 everyday objects.

Adding and subtracting

○ Find one more or one less than a number up to 10.

VOCABULARY

count, less than, more than, pair

Resources

○ Newspaper of differing sizes
○ Shoes or 'indoor shoes' or slippers or wellington boots
○ Photocopiable Sheets 5 to 7 (pages 46 to 48)
○ Number lines

Oral and mental starter

Objectives: Count reliably to 10; count in twos; count backwards from a given number

○ Play 'Take off'. The children sit in a circle and have to count around the group. When they get to 10, instead of saying '10' the child says/shouts, 'Take off', and stands up. The next child starts at 1 again and so on.

○ Play this for a while and then see if the children can play the game counting up in 2s.

○ As an extension to this, ask the children to count backwards from 10, saying 'Take off' instead of '1'.

Problem-solving challenge

How many wellies can fit on a sheet of newspaper?

With the whole class

○ For the purposes of this lesson, the problem is to do with wellington boots but it could easily be about shoes, slippers and so on.

○ Set the scene with the children by explaining how people like to put wet wellies on newspaper to dry and if you have a lot of wellies you would need a lot of newspaper!

○ With the newspaper and wellies, ask some children to come out to the front of the class and try to find different ways of putting the wellies on the newspaper. The rule is that no wellies are allowed to overlap the edges of the newspaper. Always ask the children to count how many fit on. Every time they arrange the wellies, ask lots of questions such as:

'How many wellies are there?'

'How many wellies would there be if I took 1 off?'

'How many wellies would there be if I took 2 off but then put 1 back?'

Children working in small groups

○ The children should continue to investigate how many different ways they can find of fitting the wellies on the newspaper. In the first instance, give them tabloid-sized newspapers to work with. Later, you can give them broadsheet papers. Encourage them to think of 'more than' and 'less than' questions and statements about the activity. For example:

'If I fit the boots round this way, there are more on the paper than if I fit them this way.'

'Are there less wellies on that paper than on this one?'

○ When the children have explored the possibilities, give them the relevant photocopiable sheet from pages 46 to 48. Tell them they are to count the number of wellies on each sheet of newspaper and write the answers in the boxes. These activities will act as a guide to assessing the children's ability to count to 10 reliably.

○ Where necessary, you may need to help children with their recording. An alternative is to organise the children into maths pairs and let them discuss the problem and one of them record the answer.

Note
Have a number line on display for the children to refer to. Let them come and count along it if they need to.

Plenary

○ Ask each group of children what strategies they used to try and fit the wellies on the sheet of newspaper. Ask them to say some of their 'more than' and 'less than' questions and statements.

○ Explain to the children what a pair is. Give them some questions relating to pairs and let them discuss in pairs (!) the answer to, for example:

'How many pairs of wellies would there be if we had four wellies?'

Support

○ The best way to support the less able in this lesson is to group them with other, more able children who can help them with the counting if necessary. It is important to ensure that any more able children are not dominating the group.

○ These children should work in pairs or small groups and complete photocopiable Sheet 5.

Extension

○ Ask the children to investigate how many pairs of wellies could fit on the newspaper.

○ These children should be able to work independently and complete photocopiable Sheet 7.

Questions to guide assessment

○ Could the children count their wellies accurately?
○ Did they work cooperatively?
○ Could they explain their methods and how they solved the problem?
○ Could they think of key questions?

Sort the class

Framework for Numeracy objectives

Solving problems: Reasoning about numbers or shapes
○ Sort and match objects, pictures or the children themselves, justifying the decisions made.

Counting and recognising numbers
○ Count reliably up to 10 everyday objects.

VOCABULARY

count, equals, less, match, more, sort

Resources
○ Children!
○ Objects to match
○ 10 pencils, 8 rulers and so on
○ Photocopiable sheets 8 to 10 (pages 49 to 51)

Oral and mental starter

Objective: Begin to relate addition to combining two groups of objects and then counting all the objects, then extend to three groups of objects

○ Ask four children to come out and stand in two groups of two. Ask the class to count how many children are in the two groups.

○ Explain that another way to find the answer would have been to say, '2 add 2 equals 4'.

○ Repeat this with other groups of two and then extend it to groups of three.

Problem-solving challenge

How can we 'sort' out our class?

With the whole class

○ This lesson may need to be done in the hall or other large space.

○ Without telling the children, choose a criterion such as brown hair and, name by name, ask all the children with brown hair to stand up and put themselves into a group. Ask the rest of the class:

'Why have I chosen all these children?'

○ Be prepared for some interesting answers! You will probably have to give them lots of helpful hints.

○ When, the children eventually guess the criterion, ask how many children are in this group. If the number of children is large, help with the counting.

○ Repeat this activity with lots of other 'secret' criteria – for example, the colour of tops, trousers or skirts.

○ Explain to the children that you have been doing something called 'sorting'.

○ Ask a child to come out and whisper a secret criterion to you and then choose children that match it to stand up. Beware of any criteria that may be offensive, such as 'fat children' or 'children I don't like'. Repeat this sorting activity with other criteria.

○ Stand up and tell the children that you are a group of one! Ask them to think of what criteria there might be for you being a group of one – for example, you are an adult.

○ Explain that you are going to work together to 'match' some objects to some children. Ask a group of children to hand out objects such as pencils. Make sure that there are fewer pencils than there are children. Ask questions such as:

'How many more pencils do we need so that everyone can have a pencil?'

○ Repeat this with different objects, varying the number of objects, sometimes having more objects than children. All the time, encourage the children to use the correct language, for example 'more than' and 'less than'. For example:

'There are more children than pencils.'

Children working in small groups

○ Give the children the relevant photocopiable sheet from pages 49 to 51. They have to match the groups of numbers by drawing lines.

○ These sheets can then act as an individual assessment.

Plenary

○ Without telling the children what they are, choose two criteria, for example blonde hair and glasses. Ask those children who fit these criteria to stand up. Ask the class if they can guess why these children are standing up. Explain what you have done and ask someone if they can come out and choose two secret criteria as before.

○ Remind the children what the words 'sort' and 'match' mean. Ask:

'Richard, can you match three pencils to some children so the children have one each?'

'Maya, can you sort the crayons into a red pile and a blue pile?'

Support

○ For the first part of the lesson, ask a child to come to you and whisper to them a criterion and then help them to choose the children that fit that criterion.

○ In the matching part of the lesson, involve the children by targeted questioning, for example:

'Do you think that is more than or less than?'

○ These children can then complete photocopiable Sheet 8.

Extension

○ Encourage the children to think of a really hard criterion for sorting children, such as boys with brown hair and brown eyes. Ask targeted questions to challenge them, such as:

'What would the number be if it was twice as many?'

○ These children can then complete photocopiable Sheet 10.

Questions to guide assessment

○ Could the children count reliably?
○ Could the children sort by one criterion?
○ Could the children match one-to-one?

How big is big?

Framework for Numeracy objectives

Solving problems: Problems involving 'real life' or money

○ Use developing mathematical ideas and methods to solve practical problems involving counting and comparing in a real or role-play situation.

Measures, shape and space

○ Use language such as 'more or less', 'longer or shorter', 'heavier or lighter' to compare two quantities.

VOCABULARY

bigger, biggest, longer, longest, smaller, smallest, thinner, thinnest, thicker, thickest, taller, tallest, wider, widest

Resources

○ Vocabulary cards made from photocopiable Sheet 11 on page 52
○ Objects to compare
○ Photocopiable Sheet 12 (page 53)

Oral and mental starter

Objective: Count in twos

○ Sit the children in a circle and ask them to count around the group in ones. Let them count as high as they can cope with. Repeat this, but this time every time a child counts a multiple of two that child has to stand up. With the children still standing up, get the class to just count those children standing up in twos.

○ Repeat this with the 'twos' children standing up as fast as they can.

Problem-solving challenge

What is the biggest thing in the school?

With the whole class

○ Tell the children that they are going to decide what is the biggest thing in the school. What do they think 'biggest' means?

○ First talk about longest and tallest. Show them two objects, such as a teaspoon and a fork, and ask:

'Which one is longer?'

When they are agreed, find the vocabulary card (from sheet 11, page 52) that says 'longer' and show it to them.

○ Add a wooden spoon to the teaspoon and fork. Ask:

'Which one is the longest?'

Explain that when there are two we say 'longer', but when there are more than two we say 'longest'. Find the vocabulary card.

○ Ask two children to stand up. Ask:

'Who is the taller?'

○ Ask another child to stand up. Ask:

'Who is the tallest?'

Again, explain that when there are two we say 'taller', but when there are more than two we say 'tallest'. Find the vocabulary card.

○ Introduce the words 'wider' and 'widest' using objects such as tables or spaces between objects to demonstrate what these mean.

○ Now introduce the idea of 'big'. What do the children think of as 'big'? (Buildings, aeroplanes, dinosaurs, elephants and so on?) Talk about 'bigger' and 'biggest'. Explain that it is not necessarily the tallest, or the longest, or the widest.

Children working in small groups

○ Tell the children that they are going to work in pairs to discuss what they think is the biggest thing in the classroom and then the biggest thing in the school. They can record what they think in words, drawings, or both, on Sheet 12 (page 53). Tell them to keep their decisions a secret from the other pairs.

Plenary

○ Ask all the children to fold their sheets in half and hold up the half that shows what they think is the biggest thing in the classroom. Ask individuals why they think this. Encourage them to use the correct vocabulary and hold up the vocabulary cards as they do so. For example:

'Did you think the blackboard is biggest because it is widest or tallest?'

○ Then ask the children to hold up the halves of their sheets that show what they think is the biggest thing in the school. How many agree? Take them on a walk around the school to try to find the biggest thing. When you have found it and agreed that it is, ask:

'Was anyone right?'

○ When you are all back in the classroom, discuss the different words the children have been using. Talk about how the words 'bigger' and 'biggest' are not very specific and that terms like 'taller' or 'wider' are often more appropriate.

○ Introduce the vocabulary cards that they haven't so far used. Talk about the words and what they mean.

○ Give the children a challenge to think about for tomorrow:

'What do you think is the biggest thing in the world?'

Support

○ Give the children cards made from photocopiable Sheet 11 (page 52). They put the cards face down and play a game where they turn two cards over and match them, for example 'taller' and 'tallest'. If you have a classroom assistant he or she could use the cards as 'flash' cards for the children to read out.

Extension

○ Challenge the children to say exactly what certain words mean, for example:

'What does "tall" mean?'

Questions to guide assessment

○ Could the children use the correct vocabulary?
○ Could the children compare accurately?
○ Did the children work cooperatively to tackle the problems?

Can you guess?

Framework for Numeracy objectives

Solving problems: Reasoning about numbers or shapes

○ Make simple estimates and predictions, for example, of the number of cubes that will fit in a box or strides across the room.

Counting and recognising numbers

○ Estimate a number in a range that can be counted reliably, check by counting.
○ Write numerals to 10.

> ### VOCABULARY
> count, estimate, less than, more than

Resources

○ A range of objects that the children can estimate, such as cubes, dominoes, dice, 'real' things like conkers and pebbles
○ A jar with cubes in
○ Photocopiable Sheet 13 (page 54)

Oral and mental starter

Objective: Begin to relate subtraction to 'taking away' and counting how many are left

○ Play 'Human take away!' Ask a group of four children to stand up. Then take away one member of the group. Say, 'I am now going to take away (child's name)'. Ask, 'How many are left?' Repeat this with larger groups and taking away more than one child.

Problem-solving challenge

> *How good are we at guessing?*

With the whole class

○ Ask the children if anyone knows what an estimate is. Explain that it is like a guess, only better!

○ Choose something in the classroom, such as the bookshelf, and ask the children to turn to the person next to them and guess how many books there are on the bookshelf. Give them a minute or so to do this, then ask them questions such as:

'How many of you think there are more than 20?'

'How many of you think there are less than 10,000?'

○ Discuss with the children the strategies they used to estimate. Did they just guess or did they have a strategy? Tell them about a strategy you might use. For example, you might have counted to the first five books, looked to see how much of the shelf they took and then doubled or multiplied by 4. (We are not expecting the children to multiply at this stage but showing them that there can be strategies for estimating rather than making wild guesses.)

○ Now ask them to turn to their partner and discuss how many steps it would take to walk across the room. Again, give them a minute or so to do this. Then ask the children what their estimates were. Ask how they worked out their estimates. Choose some children to walk across the room from one side to the other. The rest of the class should count aloud how many steps it took. Discuss why the number of steps was different for some children.

Children working in pairs

○ Place a number of things for the children to estimate on their tables. Give out copies of Sheet 13 (page 54). Tell the children that they have to choose an object and draw that object in the first box in the left-hand column. They then have to estimate how many of each object they can hold in one hand and write or draw their estimate on the activity sheet. Then they have to pick up as many objects as they can, then count them and write or draw how many they actually could hold. An example has been done on the sheet to show them what to do.

Plenary

○ Ask the children what objects they found most difficult to estimate and why. Ask what strategies they used to estimate.

○ Show the children the jar with cubes in it and ask them to estimate how many cubes there are. Ask a few children what their estimate is and then count out the cubes with the children counting as well.

○ Play 'Silly estimates'. Ask questions such as:

'How many fish are there in the sea?'

'How many hairs are there on Monique's head?'

'How many clouds are there in the sky?'

○ Explain that for some things it is just impossible to know how many there are.

○ Ask the children how many times they think you can say 'peanuts' in one minute. Once a few of them have given their estimates, see how many times you can say it!

Support

○ Ensure that the objects are large enough so that the children cannot hold many and therefore the number will be small.
○ Limit the number of objects the children are allowed to use.
○ To help with recording, the children could draw the objects instead of writing numbers.

Extension

○ Challenge the children to estimate how many objects they could hold in both hands.
○ Give the children smaller objects, such as counters, which will allow them to make larger estimates.

Questions to guide assessment

○ Did the children use strategies to estimate?
○ Could the children count the cubes accurately?
○ Did the children record the estimate and answer with the correct numeral(s)?
○ Did the children work cooperatively?

Get on the bus!

Framework for Numeracy objectives

Solving problems: Problems involving 'real life' or money

O Use developing mathematical ideas and methods to solve practical problems.

Counting and recognising numbers

O Begin to record numbers, initially by making marks progressing to simple tallying and writing numerals.

Adding and subtracting

O Find one more or one less than a number from 1 to 10.

VOCABULARY

more than, less than, add, subtract, equals, total

Resources

O Whiteboards and pens, or paper and pencils
O PE mat
O Number fans
O Photocopiable Sheets 14 to 17 (pages 55 to 58)
O Number lines

Oral and mental starter

Objective: Find one more or one less than a number from 1 to 10

O Play the 'I'm thinking of a number' game. Say to the children, 'I'm thinking of a number that is 1 more than 5'. The children respond with number fans. Repeat this with other numbers. To extend this activity, try numbers that are 2 more/less.

O To give the children time to think, tell them that they have to hold their fans up after you have said 'fish and chips' three times!

Problem-solving challenge

How many people will fit on the bus?

With the whole class

O Arrange the children in a circle with a PE mat in the middle of the circle. They can work in pairs recording with either the whiteboard or paper. Tell them to close their eyes, then say that the mat has now changed into the class bus! Ask them to estimate how many children they think will fit on the bus? They should write down their estimates and hold them up to show you. Discuss the range of estimates they have written. Ask them how they thought of their estimate. Then ask them one by one to sit on the 'bus' until it is full. Count how many children are on the 'bus'. Were any of the estimates right? Give the children a huge clap!

O Tell all the children to go back to their seats or get off the 'bus' and sit on the floor. Ask two children to get on the 'bus'. Instruct the other children to write something down on their whiteboards or paper that shows how many children are on the bus. Let the children record in any way they feel appropriate. Ask them to show you how they recorded, commenting on appropriate ways. Explain that the bus is off to the next stop!

O Choose another child to get on the 'bus'. Ask the rest of the class to record what has happened. Obviously, you would want them to record 2 + 1, but accept other ways. Ask them to close their eyes while you choose another child to get on the 'bus'. The rest of the class should open their eyes and then record what has happened. Continue like this until the 'bus' is full. Encourage the children to add by starting with the larger number and counting on.

O Now reverse the process with children getting off the bus and recording what happens.

Children working in groups

○ Give the children the relevant sheet for their level of ability from Sheets 14 to 16 (pages 55 to 57). This sheet asks them to record simple additions in numbers. Make sure there is a number line on display for them to use to help them do this. Encourage them to start with the large number and count on the number of people at the bus stop.

○ These activity sheets can be used for individual assessment.

○ Photocopiable Sheet 17 (page 58) is blank so that those children who are able can make up their own problems.

Plenary

○ Demonstrate on the board how to write something like 2 + 1 =. Use the correct language but also ask what other words the children know that mean the same thing. You could start with using stick men, such as below:

○ Tell the children that there are a certain number of passengers on the bus. Ask them how many there would be if there were two full buses. Let them discuss in pairs how they would solve the problem. Do not be too concerned about the correct answer at this stage. Ask them what method they would use to try to answer this question.

Support

○ Allow the children to record in any way they like, but try to encourage them to think of ways that are fairly quick.

○ Give these children photocopiable Sheet 14 and let them use cubes to help them if necessary.

Extension

○ Encourage the children to record in number sentences with the correct operation sign and the equals sign if appropriate. More able children could record two children getting on and off the bus.

○ Give these children photocopiable Sheet 16 and the blank photocopiable Sheet 17 for them to write their own problems.

Questions to guide assessment

○ Could the children record in appropriate ways?
○ Could they write their numerals correctly?
○ Could they say the number words correctly?
○ Could the children discuss with each other?

Make 10!

Framework for Numeracy objectives

Solving problems: Making decisions

○ Choose and use appropriate number operations and mental strategies to solve problems.

Calculations

○ Use knowledge that addition can be done in any order to do mental calculations more efficiently.

○ Begin to recognise that more than two numbers can be added together.

VOCABULARY

add, addition, plus, ten, zero

Resources

○ OHP
○ Number fans
○ 10 objects, small enough to have several at once on an OHP
○ Photocopiable Sheets 18 to 19 (pages 59 to 60)
○ Cubes
○ Number lines

Oral and mental starter

Objective: Count reliably up to 10 objects (revision)

○ Put some objects on the OHP. Ask the children to hold up their number fans to show you the number of objects you have put on the OHP.

○ Vary the amount of time the children are allowed to count the objects to encourage accuracy.

○ Sometimes put the objects in an ordered manner – this will help develop the children's mental imagery. For example:

Problem-solving challenge

How many different ways can we add up to 10?

With the whole class

○ Draw a square on the board with circles in the corners. Write a big 10 in the middle of the square. Ask the children to think of four digits that could be put in the circles so that when they are added together they equal 10 – for example, 2, 2, 2 and 4. For this challenge, they are not allowed to use zero.

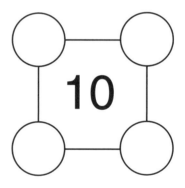

○ Talk to the children about how they could check that the answer is correct. One good strategy is to add the numbers more than once and each time in a different order. Stress how important it is to check your answers.

○ Repeat this with another four digits.

Children working as individuals

○ Give the children copies of Sheet 18 (page 59). Tell them that they have to find as many different ways as they can of making 10 by adding up four digits and then record them on the sheet. Encourage them to try to do this activity mentally, with jottings if necessary. Ask them how many different ways they think there are.

○ At first glance, it would appear that there are a lot of solutions to this problem but in fact there are not. The solutions are:

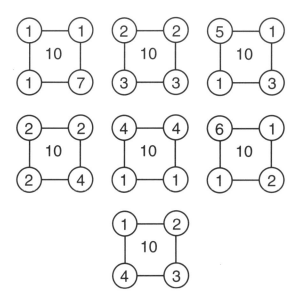

The children will have many repetitions.

Support

○ Let the children use materials to support their addition. They could use cubes or a number line to help them.

○ The challenge could also be simplified by allowing the children to use zero.

Extension

○ Give these children photocopiable Sheet 19 with a number between 10 and 20 in the square. What four numbers can they put in the circles to add up to the number in the square. How many different sets of numbers are there?

Questions to guide assessment

○ Could the children add the numbers up mentally?
○ Did the children check their answers and, if so, how?
○ Did the children have a strategy to try to find as many ways as they could?
○ Did the children reflect on the problem?

Plenary

○ Ask the children questions such as the following.

'How many different ways of making 10 did you find?'

'Are you sure they are all different?'

'What strategies did you use?'

'How can we be sure that we have found all the ways?'

'Did you check your answers and, if so, how?'

Write their answers and some of their strategies on the board.

Making money

Framework for Numeracy objectives

Solving problems: Problems involving 'real life', money or measures

○ Use mental strategies to solve simple problems set in 'real life' money or measurement contexts, using counting, addition, subtraction, doubling and halving, explaining methods and reasoning orally.

○ Recognise coins of different values.

Calculations

○ Begin to use the addition and equals signs to record mental calculations.

> **VOCABULARY**
>
> check, count, cube, different, how many?, square, ten

Resources

○ OHP and OHP calculator
○ Coins
○ Large demonstration coins
○ Photocopiable Sheet 20 (page 61)

Oral and mental starter

Objective: Count on in ones from any small number

○ Set up the OHP calculator to count up in 1s.
Press $\boxed{1}\boxed{+}\boxed{1}\boxed{=}\boxed{=}\boxed{=}$ or $\boxed{1}\boxed{+}\boxed{+}\boxed{1}\boxed{=}\boxed{=}\boxed{=}$

○ Choose a child to press the equals button. The rest of the class have to say the next number before the button is pressed. Try this with start numbers from 1 to 10.

○ Split the class into small groups and repeat the activity but with each group saying the number in turn.

Problem-solving challenge

> *How many different ways can we pay 5p? 10p? 20p? 50p?*

With the whole class

○ Using either large demonstration coins or real coins, ask the children to tell you what each coin is worth. Write 5p on the board and then ask the children:

'If I were to buy a sweet and it cost 5p, how many different coins could I use to pay for it?'

○ Let the children discuss this in pairs using real coins and jotting down their answers.

○ Then ask some children to come out and write their answers on the board. Let them record this in any way they want, but point out that one way to record it would be like this: 2p + 2p + 1p = 5p.

○ When you have some answers on the board, give the children some time to see if they can find any other ways that are not on the board. Ask some of them to write on the board the other ways they have found.

○ Talk to the children about having a logical approach to solving this problem. Ask:

'What might be a way to find all the different ways using 2ps?'

Children working as individuals/pairs

○ Ask the children to repeat this activity with sweets costing 10p, 20p and 50p.

○ Give them copies of Sheet 20 (page 61) with a suitable coin value written in at the top of the sheet. They need to draw the coins that make up that amount in the boxes. So, if the coin amount they have been given is 20p, they might complete their sheet as shown in the example below.

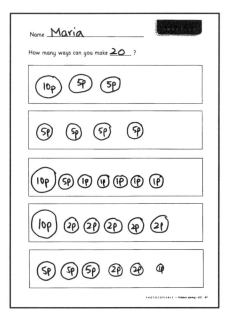

Alternatively, they might record in the rectangles as if they were calculations:

5p + 5p + 5p + 5p = 20p

Plenary

○ Emphasise the importance of having a good strategy to solve problems like this. Ask the children what strategies they used and if they worked!

○ Finish the lesson by giving the children some money problems such as:

'If a sweet costs 19p and you have a 20p coin, how much change will you get?'

'If a sweet costs 16p and you have a 20p coin, how much change will you get?'

Support

○ Some children will need to spend a lot of time practising ways to pay for something that costs 5p. Encourage them to adopt a logical approach. One way to help them develop this is for them to 'sort' their answers in some way. For example, all the ways starting with 1p.

○ Some children will also need support on recording the different answers. One way to do this is for the children to draw around the coins in their answers and write the coin amount in the coin. If you have cardboard coins, you could get the children to stick the coins on to paper with Blu-tack.

Extension

○ Challenge more able children to investigate ways of buying something that costs 50p or even £1. With these children, encourage them to record in an appropriate way – using addition and equals signs. They should also be encouraged to think of a logical approach to solving the problem.

Questions to guide assessment

○ Could the children use mental strategies to solve these problems?

○ Could they add up the coins accurately?

○ Could they work cooperatively to solve the problem?

Let's talk about veg!

Framework for Numeracy objectives

Solving problems: Problems involving 'real life', money or measures

○ Use mental strategies to solve simple problems set in 'real life' money or measurement contexts, using counting, addition, subtraction, doubling and halving, explaining methods and reasoning orally.

Measures, shape and space

○ Compare two lengths, masses or capacities by direct comparison; extend to more than two.
○ Understand and use the vocabulary related to length, mass and capacity.
○ Measure using uniform non-standard units or standard units.

VOCABULARY

longest, shortest, heaviest, lightest, fastest, slowest

Resources

○ Whiteboards
○ A range of vegetables
○ Measuring equipment
○ Weights

Oral and mental starter

Objective: Read and write numerals to at least 10

○ With the children recording on whiteboards, ask the children to write down the numbers you say and then hold them up.

○ Write the numbers 1 to 10 on the board. As you point at them, the children have to say the numbers. To liven up this activity, get the children to shout or whisper the numbers!

Problem-solving challenge

How long is a carrot?

With the whole class

○ Put a range of vegetables on each of the children's tables. Explain that today they are going to investigate vegetables! Either have the following questions written on the board or ask the children:

'Which vegetable is the longest?'

'Which vegetable is the heaviest?'

'Which vegetable is the lightest?'

'Which vegetable can roll the furthest?'

'Which vegetable can spin for the longest time?'

○ Ask the children if they can think of any other questions they would like to find the answer to. Write those on the board.

○ Tell the children they are now going to work in groups to find the answers to these questions.

Children working in groups

○ Put a collection of vegetables on each group's table. Choose one of the questions and ask the children to go to their tables and, by comparing the vegetables on their table, select one vegetable that is the longest, or whichever criterion you have chosen. When they are agreed, one person in each group should bring that vegetable out to you.

○ Once every group has brought out their vegetable, compare all of them to find out which is the longest. If there is any dispute about the 'longest', ask the children what they could measure with to solve this problem. Then let some children do the measuring. Take this opportunity to ask 'number'-related questions, such as:

'What would this leek be if it were twice as long?'

'What would this carrot be if it were half as long?'

○ Repeat this for as many vegetable comparisons as you feel is appropriate.

Plenary

○ Tell the children that the world record for the heaviest carrot was just over 10kg! If you have enough weights, put 10kg in a safe container and ask some children to see if they can lift it up!

○ Other interesting facts to use are: the heaviest beetroot was 22.25kg and the heaviest celery was 26.7kg. A giant cabbage can weigh over 41kg!

Support

○ If the children are in mixed ability groups, then the less able children will be supported by the other children. When it comes to measuring the vegetables, choose children you know will be able to measure them.

Extension

○ As you are working with the children, select the more able children to answer more challenging questions such as:

'If it was three times heavier, how heavy would it be?'

Questions to guide assessment

○ Could the children use the correct vocabulary?
○ Could they compare with some degree of accuracy?
○ Could they work cooperatively?

Triangle chop!

Framework for Numeracy objectives

Solving problems: Reasoning about numbers or shapes

○ Investigate a general statement about familiar shapes by finding examples that satisfy it.

Measures, shape and space

○ Use everyday language to describe features of familiar 3D and 2D shapes.

VOCABULARY

angle, corner, edge, side, straight, triangle

Resources

○ Whiteboards (optional)
○ Photocopiable Sheets 21 to 22 (pages 62 to 63)
○ Scissors
○ Glue
○ A3 paper

Oral and mental starter

Objective: Recall addition doubles up to 5 + 5.

○ Ask the children to write down any number from 1 to 10 on a piece of paper or whiteboard. Say that anyone who has written the double of 4 should hold up their paper/whiteboard. Tell the children that you will always be asking questions about doubles. Repeat this a number of times. If children have been writing odd numbers down, some class discussion is in order!

Problem-solving challenge

If you cut a triangle in half, do you get two more triangles?

With the whole class

○ Either hold up a large triangle or draw one on the board. Ask the children questions such as:

'What do we call this shape?'

'How many sides has it got?'

'How many corners has it got?'

○ Tell the children that you are going to give them a BIG challenge to find out about. The challenge is this – is it true that if you cut a triangle in half, you get two more triangles?

○ Ask the children to put up their hands if they agree that you would get two more triangles. Ask them to tell you why if they can. You might get some interesting answers!

○ Explain that they are going to work in groups and cut out some triangles and fold them in half. Before sending them off to their groups, talk about how you know that something is folded in half correctly.

Children working in pairs

○ Give the children copies of photocopiable Sheet 21 (page 62). They should cut out the triangles and fold them in half. What conclusions do they come to?

○ After they have done this, ask them if they can arrange some of their triangles into other shapes and stick them on paper. Tell them they will need their shapes for the plenary session.

○ The next challenge is to make as many triangles as they can from the one big triangle. Give them copies of photocopiable Sheet 22. Ask them how many triangles they think can be made. They should stick all their triangles on paper in height order.

Support

○ It may help some children if their triangles are cut out already. Then they have only to perform a fold and a straight cut.

Extension

○ When the children make other shapes, challenge them to make as many different shapes as they can. Ask them if they can name their shapes.

Plenary

○ Ask if everyone agrees that if you cut a triangle in half you always get two smaller ones.

○ Ask the children how many triangles they made from the big one.

○ Ask some of the children to show the shapes they made from their triangles.

○ Draw a star shape on the board made out of two overlapping triangles. Ask questions about the star – for example:

'How many sides has it got?'

'How many corners (angles) has it got?'

'Can anyone see a connection between the number of corners of a triangle and the number of corners in the star?' (3/6)

'Is there a connection between the number of sides of a triangle and the number of sides in the star?' (3/12)

○ Finish by asking the children to hold up their fingers to show how many sides a triangle has.

Questions to guide assessment

○ Did the children agree with the statement? If not, what were the issues?
○ What language did the children use to describe their shapes?
○ Did any children use the correct mathematical language?

It all adds up!

Framework for Numeracy objectives

Solving problems: Reasoning about numbers or shapes

○ Solve simple mathematical problems or puzzles; recognise and predict from simple patterns and relationships. Suggest extensions by asking 'What if...?' or 'What could I try next?'

Calculations

○ Use number facts to add/subtract pair of numbers mentally within the range 0 to at least 10 then 0 to at least 20.

○ Use +, – and = signs to record mental calculations in a number sentence.

VOCABULARY

add, subtract, plus, minus, equals

Resources

○ An OHP calculator
○ A class set of calculators

Oral and mental starter

Objective: Recall addition and subtraction facts for each number up to 10

○ Using an OHP calculator, enter a number from 1 to 9. Ask some children out to the front to add another number to the first so that the calculator shows 10.

○ Repeat this.

○ After a while, enter a number from 11 to 20. Ask some children to do a subtraction that will give an answer of 10.

○ Repeat this.

Problem-solving challenge

Can we choose the right number to key into a calculator to get an answer of 11?

With the whole class

○ Using either an OHP calculator or with an ordinary one, teach the children how to play '11 Up'. The rules are that two children have one calculator between them. They take it in turns to enter either + 1 or + 2 (their choice) and then press the = key. The first child to get 11 on the calculator wins the game. The challenge for the children is to find out what number they need to get to guarantee victory.

○ Having demonstrated the game, tell the children they are going to work in pairs to play the game.

Children working in pairs

○ Let the children play the game for some time.

○ Go round the pairs watching the children as they play. Discuss with them the importance of getting to 8 first. If you get to 8, your opponent cannot win. Similarly, you will win if you get to 5 and 2.

○ Once they see how it works, some children will spot that it matters who starts the game.

○ Now play '11 Down'. This game has the same rules, but the children have to subtract 1 or 2, and the first child to get to 0 wins.

○ Again, discuss with the children the number they have to get to guarantee to win.

○ Ask the children to play both games again, but this time they have to record what they entered into the calculator on paper.

Plenary

○ Using an OHP calculator play the '110 Up' game. The rules for this are just the same, but you add either 10 or 20. Discuss with the children the similarities with '11 Up'. Stress that adding with 10 and 20 is no more difficult than adding with 1 or 2.

Support

○ Draw a number track 11 squares long so that an interlocking cube will fit onto one square on the track. Get the children to join interlocking cubes into twos. They can now play the same game but with cubes. Each child takes turns to put down either a single cube or a double cube. The first child to complete the line wins.

Extension

○ Play the same game but as '21 Up' and '21 Down'.

Questions to guide assessment

○ Could the children play the game well?
○ Did they calculate mentally before using the calculator?
○ Could they record with appropriate symbols?

Mystery code cubes

Framework for Numeracy objectives

Solving problems: Reasoning about numbers or shapes
○ Solve simple mathematical problems or puzzles; recognise and predict from simple patterns and relationships. Suggest extensions by asking 'What if...? or 'What could I try next?'

Calculations
○ Add more than two numbers.
○ Use number facts to add/subtract pair of numbers within range 0 to 20.
○ Add 9 to a single–digit number by adding 10 then subtracting 1.

VOCABULARY
add, subtract, plus, minus, equals

Resources
○ Class set of calculators
○ Interlocking cubes
○ Photocopiable Sheet 23 (page 64)

Oral and mental starter

Objective: Recall pairs of numbers that total 10

○ Put the children into pairs with one calculator between them. Tell one child to enter a number between 1 and 9 on the calculator. The other child has to enter an addition so that the answer is 10. The children then take turns to do this.

Problem-solving challenge

Can we work out what value the cubes represent?

With the whole class

○ Before the lesson, choose five different coloured cubes and put them in a bag. Allocate the following values to each of the cubes: +/–6, +/–7, +/–8, +/–9, +/–10. So the red cube is +6 or –6, the green cube +7 or –7 and so on. The children must not know the values you have allocated to the cubes.

○ Ask the children to give you a number from 1 to 10. Write this on the board. Now get one of the cubes out of the bag and show it to the children so that they can see the colour. Write the colour of the cube on the board and the number you have when the value of the cube has been added to the number you initially wrote on the board. Still don't say anything to the children.

○ Put the cube back in the bag and repeat the activity with a different start number. As you keep doing this you should be completing a chart like the one below.

Start number	Colour of cube	End number
5	red	11
2	blue	12
3	green	10

○ At some point, tell the children they have to work out what the cubes are doing to the start number. Can they see that each cube has been allocated a value for addition?

○ Now introduce the subtraction value for the cubes so that each cube now has two values. Once the children have worked out the value of each cube, hold up the '9' cube. Show the children how to add 9 by adding 10 and taking away 1.

Children working in pairs

○ The children can now do the same activity in pairs. Each child chooses five cubes and gives them different values to those you gave them. The child who has given the cubes their values records the results on Sheet 23 (page 64). Their partner has to guess the value of each cube.

Plenary

○ Ask the children to sit in a circle and use the five original cubes. Choose a child to start and give them a start number, such as 3. Pull out a cube and say this is add and whatever value it is. The child has to add the value to the start number and say the answer to the person next to them. Repeat this for the next child, but as a subtraction. Carry on around the group like this. When the '9' cube comes out, repeat about how to do this by adding 10 and taking away 1.

Support

○ Let the children work with fewer cubes and use smaller numbers – for example, 1 to 3.

○ Instead of two values, let the children just use addition.

○ It may help to let the children use number lines to work out the answers.

Extension

○ Let the children use bigger numbers, say 10 to 15.

Questions to guide assessment

○ Could the children do the additions and subtractions mentally?
○ Which children used the strategy of adding 10 and taking off 1?

Our school shop

Framework for Numeracy objectives

Solving problems: Problems involving 'real life' money or measures

○ Use mental strategies to solve simple word problems using one or two steps. Explain how the problem was solved.

○ Recognise all coins and begin to use £.p notation for money (for example, know that £4.65 indicates £4 and 65p).

○ Find totals, give change and work out which coins to pay.

Calculations

○ Use knowledge that addition can be done in any order to do mental calculations more efficiently.

○ Understand that more than two numbers can be added.

○ Begin to add three single-digit numbers mentally (totals up to about 20) or three two-digit numbers with the help of apparatus (totals up to 100).

○ Check results of calculations – repeat addition in a different order.

VOCABULARY

add, addition, minus, plus, subtraction, take away

Resources

○ OHP calculator
○ Photocopiable Sheets 24 to 25 (pages 65 to 66)
○ Coins
○ A3 size copy of Sheet 24 for the plenary
○ Structural apparatus
○ Number lines
○ 100 squares

Oral and mental starter

Objective: Say the number names to at least 100

○ Using an OHP calculator invite some children to enter a TU number. They then ask the class what that number is. The class has to say the number out loud after a count of 3 (to allow the less able children to feel less threatened by the activity). Repeat this.

Problem-solving challenge

What's the most I can get for £1?

With the whole class

○ Tell the children you are feeling very kind today and that you are going to give them all £1 to spend! Say that they will be working with a partner and have to 'buy' as many different things as they can from the school shop for that £1. They will have to write down the different combinations of food they can buy, how much it would cost, what coins they would use and how much change from a pound they would get.

○ Talk to them about sensible strategies for adding up. For example, it does not matter which order you add numbers up in, the answer will still be the same, but it is sensible to start with the larger number and add on the smaller numbers.

○ Remind the children of the need to check their calculations and that adding the numbers in a different order is one way.

○ Talk to them about how to work out how much change they should get – counting on would be one good strategy. Demonstrate this on the board.

Children working in pairs

○ Organise the children into their pairs and give each pair a copy of photocopiable Sheets 24 and 25 (pages 65 to 66). Sheet 24 shows the items that are available to purchase from the shop and Sheet 25 is a recording sheet. (This can either be used for two different transactions, or cut in two for one transaction.)

Plenary

○ Ask questions such as:

'How many different ways did you find to spend your £1?'

'Did anyone spend exactly £1 and, if so, how did you do it?'

'What ways did you add the numbers up?'

○ Say to the children:

'If I gave you 10 times more money, how much money would I give you?'

○ Refer to the A3 copy of Sheet 24 and ask the children,

'If all these prices were 10 times bigger, how much would each item be?'

Discuss ways to work out this increase.

Support

○ Limit the number of items the children can buy from the shop. Tell them they can only buy, for example, two items, and they have to work out the cost of those. Support them by supplying appropriate apparatus.

Extension

○ How many different items can the children buy so that the total spent is exactly £1? Encourage the children to calculate as much as possible mentally, with jottings if appropriate.

Questions to guide assessment

○ Could the children add up accurately?
○ Did they add up mentally or did they use apparatus – cubes/number lines?
○ Did they check their calculations?
○ What strategies did they use to choose the items to buy? For example, all sweets!

Just 1 and 2 – that's the lot!

Framework for Numeracy objectives

Solving problems: Making decisions
○ Choose and use appropriate operations and efficient calculation strategies (such as mental, mental with jottings) to solve problems.

Calculations
○ Extend understanding of the operations of addition and subtraction.
○ Use and begin to read the related vocabulary. Use the +, – and = signs to record mental additions and subtractions in a number sentence, and recognise the use of a symbol such as ❏ or △ to stand for an unknown number. Recognise that addition can be done in any order, but not subtraction. For example, $3 + 21 = 21 + 3$, but $21 – 3$ does not equal $3 – 21$.
○ Understand that more than two numbers can be added.
○ Begin to add three single-digit numbers mentally (totals up to about 20) or three two-digit numbers with the help of apparatus (totals up to 100).

VOCABULARY
add, addition, make, more, plus, sum, total

Resources
○ Structural apparatus
○ Number lines
○ 100 squares

Oral and mental starter

Objective: Count on or back in ones from any number

○ Sit the children in a circle. Give the first child a start number and ask the rest to count up in ones. Then tell them they have to watch you because when your hand goes up that means they have to count in their heads until your hand comes down when they can count aloud again. After a while introduce another signal – when you stand up, the count has to go down in ones. Combine both signals for most fun!

Problem-solving challenge

> *How many different numbers can I get using just the digits 1 and 2?*

With the whole class

○ Tell the children that they are going to use the digits 1 and 2 to make as many different numbers as they can. They must use only those digits but they can use them as often as they like. They can add or subtract them. The challenge is to find as many different numbers as they can. Give an easy example on the board and let them come and do some examples on the board as well.

$1 + 2 = 3$	$2 – 1 = 1$
$11 + 2 = 13$	$11 – 2 = 9$
$1 + 22 = 23$	$22 – 1 = 21$
and so on	

Children working individually

❍ Let the children tackle this problem with the minimum of guidance initially. Stop them after a while and ask what numbers they have got. Write those numbers on the board. When you have got all the answers so far, invite a child to put the numbers in order, smallest first. Ask the children to try to find the 'missing' numbers. Ask them what strategies they are using to find as many answers as they can.

❍ After a while, stop the children and ask if anyone has put the 1 and 2 together to make 12? Ask 'What other tens and unit numbers could we make by combining 1 and 2?' (11, 21, 22)

❍ Now the children may need to use apparatus of some kind to help solve the calculations – number lines and 100 squares would be very useful.

❍ Tell the children to look for their most complicated answer so it can be used in the plenary.

Plenary

❍ Refer back to the list of numbers on the board and ask for any other numbers to be added to it. Ask questions about the numbers such as:

'What is the highest number?'
'What is the lowest number?'

❍ Pointing to two numbers, ask:

'What numbers are between these two?'

❍ Ask the children for their most complicated answer and choose someone to write it on the board. Ask how they know the answer is right and how they worked it out.

Support

❍ In an open-ended investigation such as this, the less able children should be able to cope with the activity but may need support in terms of apparatus of some description. Encourage the children to use jottings as an aid to their calculations.

Extension

❍ Encourage the children to find long and complicated answers! Give the children target numbers such as 50 or 100. Can they get those numbers just using 1 and 2? If they can, how many ways can they find?

❍ If the children have had experience of negative numbers, they could try to find answers that are negative.

Questions to guide assessment

❍ Could the children cope with the activity?
❍ Did the children use mental methods with or without jottings?
❍ If the children used apparatus, what did they use?
❍ Did children tackle the problem in a systematic way or randomly?

It's about time!

Framework for Numeracy objectives

Solving problems: Problems involving 'real life' money or measures

○ Use mental addition and subtraction, simple multiplication and division, to solve simple word problems involving numbers in 'real life', money or measures, using one or two steps.

○ Explain how the problem was solved.

Measures, shape and space

○ Use and begin to read the vocabulary related to time.

○ Use units of time and know the relationships between them (second, minute, hour, day, week).

○ Suggest suitable units to estimate or measure time.

○ Order the months of the year.

VOCABULARY

seconds, minutes, hours, days, weeks, years

Resources

○ Number fans
○ Rulers
○ Pencils
○ Books
○ Timing devices (stopwatch, clock, sand timer)
○ Number lines
○ 100 squares
○ Photocopiable Sheets 26 to 29 (pages 67 to 70)

Oral and mental starter

Objective: Say the number that is one or ten more/less than a two-digit number

○ Ask children questions related to time such as these:
'How many days in a week?'
'How many seconds in a minute?'
'How many hours in a day?'
'How many minutes in an hour?'
Children respond with number fans. After each question, ask questions such as:
'What is 1 more (or less) than that number?'
'What is 10 more (or less) than that number?'

Problem-solving challenge

For how long can you balance a pencil on one finger?

With the whole class

○ Tell the children that they are going to be working on estimates. Do they know what 'estimate' means? Ask someone to give you a definition.

○ Hand out copies of photocopiable Sheet 26 (page 67). Read it through with them. Explain that they have to think carefully about the questions and then fill in their estimates for each one. They should write whether they think it is seconds, minutes or even hours! They should aim to be as accurate as possible.

○ Once all the children have written their estimates, organise them into pairs. Tell them they are going to find out how accurate their estimates were.

Children working in pairs

○ They should take it in turns to do each activity while their partner times them. They then write the actual time taken on Sheet 26 in the space provided.

○ Now give the children photocopiable Sheets 27 and 28. Now the aim is to use their findings to undertake another exercise. Explain that they have to find the difference between their estimate and the actual time taken. They should write out their calculations in the boxes. Let them use any apparatus they want to solve these problems. For example, one answer might be:

Estimate   = 22 seconds
Actual   = 19 seconds
Difference = 22 – 19 = 3 seconds

○ Talk to the children about their estimates.

'How close were your estimates?'

'What was your closest estimate?'

'Was anyone a long way out with any estimates?

Plenary

○ Talk to the children about the different ways they solved the problems.

○ Cut out the cards on photocopiable Sheet 29 (page 70). Ask 12 children to stand together at the front of the class, and give each a card but not in the correct month order. Ask the rest of the class to estimate how long it will take the 12 children to get into correct month order. Write a few estimates on the board. Time the 12 children as they get into order. Repeat this with another 12 children.

Support

○ Talk to the children about their estimates to ensure that they are reasonably accurate. If they are not, help them to refine these estimates. You may want to pair children in such a way that a more able child works with a less able one.

○ For photocopiable Sheets 27 and 28, provide apparatus to help the children solve the problems.

Extension

○ For photocopiable Sheets 27 and 28, you can extend the work by asking the children to see if they can double/halve their answers.

○ Challenge these children to do all the calculations mentally.

Questions to guide assessment

○ How accurate were the estimates?
○ What methods did the children use to calculate?
○ Could the children work in a cooperative way?

Make me square!

Framework for Numeracy objectives

Solving problems: Reasoning about numbers or shapes
○ Investigate a general statement about familiar numbers or shapes by finding examples that satisfy it (or do not).

Measures, shape and space
○ Make and describe shapes, pictures and patterns using, for example, solid shapes, templates, pin-board and elastic bands, squared paper.

VOCABULARY
corner, edge, right angle, square, symmetry

Resources
○ 2D squares
○ Squared paper (see page 42)
○ OHP calculator or class set of calculators
○ Felt-tipped pens or crayons

Oral and mental starter

Objective: Recall doubles to 10 + 10 and corresponding halves

○ Ask the children to write a number between 10 and 20 on a piece of paper. Say, 'Hold up your piece of paper if your number is double 6.'

○ Repeat this for other doubles. To make it into a game, the children can give themselves a point every time they are correct. After a while, change the game so the children have to write a number between 1 and 10. Say, 'Hold up your piece of paper if your number is half of 16.' Repeat this – if children are writing down odd numbers, some discussion may be required!

Problem-solving challenge

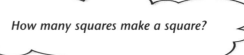
How many squares make a square?

With the whole class

○ Either with a large square shape or one that is drawn on the board, ask the children what they can tell you about a square. Points to bring out are: four sides, four corners/angles, four right angles and lines of symmetry.

○ Write on the board this statement, 'When you join squares together they will always make another, larger square.'

○ Ask the children to discuss this statement in pairs. After a short while ask,

'Who agrees with the statement and why?'

○ Tell the children that they are going to work in pairs to investigate that statement and try to prove if it is true or false.

Children working in pairs

○ Once the children have established that it is possible to make a square from certain numbers of squares, ask them to find as many squares as they can and record them on squared paper (they could use copies of page 42). Next to each drawing, ask them to write the number of squares that the bigger square is made up of.

With the whole class

○ Ask the children to tell you the number of squares in each of the larger squares they have made (4 , 9, 16, 25, 36 and so on). Explain that these are called 'square numbers'. (This is a Y5 objective, but this activity will lay a good foundation for the children.)

○ Either with the OHP calculator and/or with the children using their own calculators, show them how the square root key works. Ask them what the connection is between the square root and the squares they drew.

○ Ask the children to count the right angles in their squares and record the numbers on the board (16, 36, 64 and so on). Can they spot the connection?

Plenary

○ Refer back to the statement at the start of the lesson and ask who agrees with it. Hopefully nobody will put his or her hand up! Ask if anyone can remember the name for numbers that can be made into squares. Write on the board 'square numbers'.

○ Ask the children who looked for squares in the classroom (see Support) to show the rest of the class what they found.

Support

○ The children would benefit from using interlocking cubes to do this investigation as this eliminates many variables. Tell them that the cubes have to be fixed together. Rather than go on to the next activity, these children should spend time a) making squares b) counting right angles and c) looking for squares around the classroom.

Extension

○ To develop this activity, draw this shape on the board.

Ask the children how many squares there are in this shape (5).

○ Then draw this shape on the board.

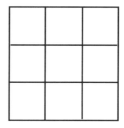

Ask the children to find as many squares as they can (14).

Up the wall!

Framework for Numeracy objectives

Solving problems: Reasoning about numbers or shapes

❍ Solve mathematical problems or puzzles, recognise simple patterns and relationships, generalise and predict. Suggest extensions by asking 'What if...?' or 'What could I try next?'

Calculations

❍ Understand that more than two numbers can be added.
❍ Begin to add three single-digit numbers mentally (totals up to about 20) or three two-digit numbers with the help of apparatus (totals up to 100).

VOCABULARY

add, addition, minus, plus, subtraction, take away

Resources

❍ Class set of calculators
❍ Photocopiable Sheets 30 to 31 (pages 71 to 72)

Oral and mental starter

Objective: Recall addition and subtraction facts for each number up to 10

❍ Ask the children to work in pairs with one calculator between them. The first child enters a number between 1 and 9, the second child has to add to that start number so that it equals 10.
❍ The first child has to enter a number between 11 and 20, the second child has to subtract a number from the start number so that it equals 10.

Problem-solving challenge

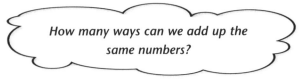

How many ways can we add up the same numbers?

With the whole class

❍ Draw a wall on the board like the one below.

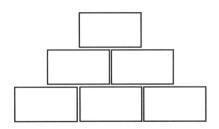

❍ Write 1, 2 and 3 in the bottom bricks. Explain to the children that you have to add the 2 numbers together to get the number for the next brick up. Do this to get the total of 8 in the top brick.

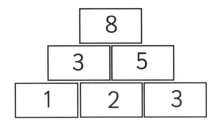

❍ Ask the children to discuss in pairs how they could put the numbers 1, 2 and 3 in a different order in the bricks so that when they add them together they get a higher total in the top brick.

❍ Ask for their suggestions and try them on the board. Ask the children why putting the 3 in the middle brick should give the highest total.

Children working individually

○ Give the children photocopiable Sheet 30 (page 71).
Ask them to find the highest total using 1, 2, 3, 4.
Tell them that they must be able to prove, in some
way, that their total is the highest. Provide paper for
them to jot numbers down.

○ Then give them Sheet 31 and ask them to get the
highest and lowest totals they can using 1, 2, 3, 4, 5.
Give them time to do this activity and then discuss
their answers and strategies.

Plenary

○ Talk to the children about the strategies they used to
find the highest and lowest totals.

○ Draw the bricks from the whole class activity on the
board again and ask for suggestions for a TU number
to go in the top brick. Then ask for suggestions for
numbers to go in the bricks below the top one and
so on. Could the numbers get to the bottom without
becoming fractions? Repeat this with other start
numbers.

Support

○ Less able children should try to find as many ways as
they can of rearranging 1, 2, 3 and 4 in the bricks.
They should be encouraged to adopt a systematic
approach to this problem.

Extension

○ A good extension challenge is to ask the children to
find a number that will go in the top brick so that it
will give numbers that will get to the bottom bricks
without becoming fractions.

Questions to guide assessment

○ Could the children add the numbers up mentally?
○ What resources did the children use to add up?
○ Did the children transfer their skills from one
problem to the next?

Getting even!

Framework for Numeracy objectives

Solving problems: Reasoning about numbers or shapes
○ Investigate a general statement about familiar numbers by finding examples that satisfy it.

Numbers and the number system
○ Recognise odd and even numbers to at least 30.

VOCABULARY
digit, even, false, odd, true

Resources
○ Photocopiable Sheets 32 to 34 (pages 73 to 75)
○ An OHP calculator or class set of calculators

Oral and mental starter

Objective: Partition a 2-digit number into tens and ones

○ Using an OHP calculator, enter a two-digit number, such as 45. Ask a volunteer to come out and remove the 4 from the screen by using subtraction. Involve the rest of the class by asking them to show with number fans what that 4 really is. The volunteer then has to remove the 5 by using subtraction. Repeat this.

Problem-solving challenge

What's different about even numbers?

With the whole class

○ Write on the board the statement, 'All even numbers end in 2, 4, 6, 8, or 0 and odd numbers do not!'

○ Give out copies of photocopiable Sheet 32 (page 73) and ask the children to colour in the number 2 and then all the numbers underneath it down to 92. Repeat this for 4, 6, 8, 0. Ask the children:

'What do we call the numbers coloured in and the numbers not coloured in?'

'What can you tell me about the end digit of the even numbers?'

'What can you tell me about the end digit of the odd numbers?'

○ Either with an OHP calculator and/or a class set of calculators, show the children how to generate the even numbers using the constant function on the calculator. Enter + 2 and keep pressing the = key. (On some calculators, you need to enter + + 2 =.) Let the children practise this on their own calculators. Then ask them to clear the calculator and enter the + 2 again. Tell them to keep going until you say 'Stop'. When you say 'Stop' ask the children:

'What is the last digit in your number?'

○ Repeat this a few times.

○ Now ask the children to enter 2 + 1 = or 2 + + 1 = and keep pressing the = key. This will give them the odd numbers. Let the children do this on their calculators. As before, tell them to stop and ask them what the last digit of their number is. Ask:

'Has anyone got a 2, 4, 6, 8 or 0 as their last digit?'

Children working individually

○ Give out copies of either photocopiable Sheet 33 or 34 (pages 74 to 75). Tell the children to write odd or even next to each number.

Plenary

○ Ask the children to tell you the difference between odd and even numbers. Then write some numbers on the board and, without the children referring to the calculator or their 100 square, ask them to say whether the numbers are odd or even. A good way to do this is to point to a number and if it is even the children hold up a thumb, if it is odd they hold up a finger and thumb. Give the children five seconds to think about it before they have to hold up a finger or thumb.

○ Finish by asking the children to say whether the statement on the board is true or false.

Support

○ Let the children start with photocopiable Sheet 34 – it would be easier for them to use the 100 square to answer the questions but they may want to use the calculator, in which case let them!

Extension

○ Let the children write down a list of 10 numbers between 100 and 200. Ask them to write next to the number whether they think it is odd or even. They can then use the calculator constant function to see whether they were correct or not.

Questions to guide assessment

○ Which way did the children use to find odd and even?
○ Could the children decide which numbers were odd and even without any support?

Name _____

Name _____

How many?

Name _____

How many?

Name _____

How many?

Name _____

How many?

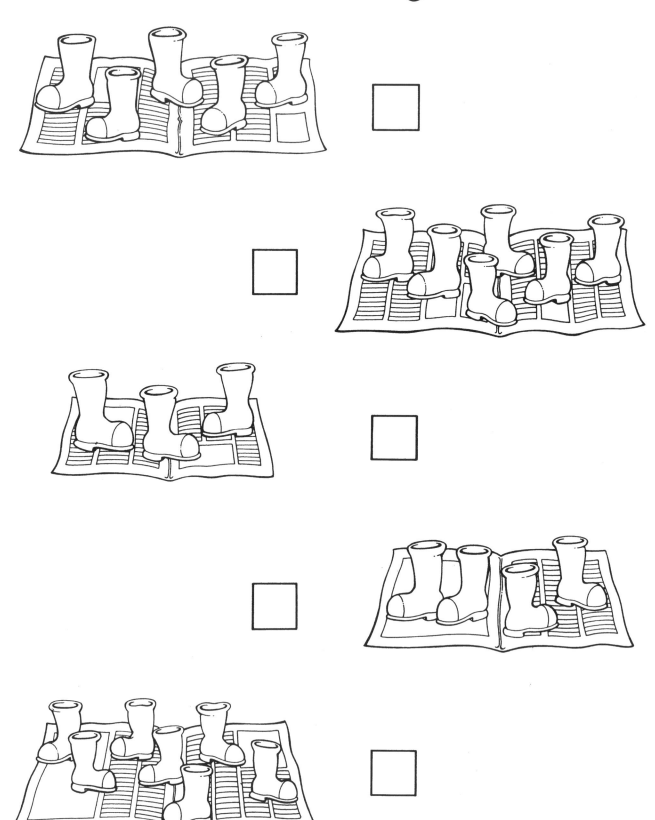

Name _____

How many?

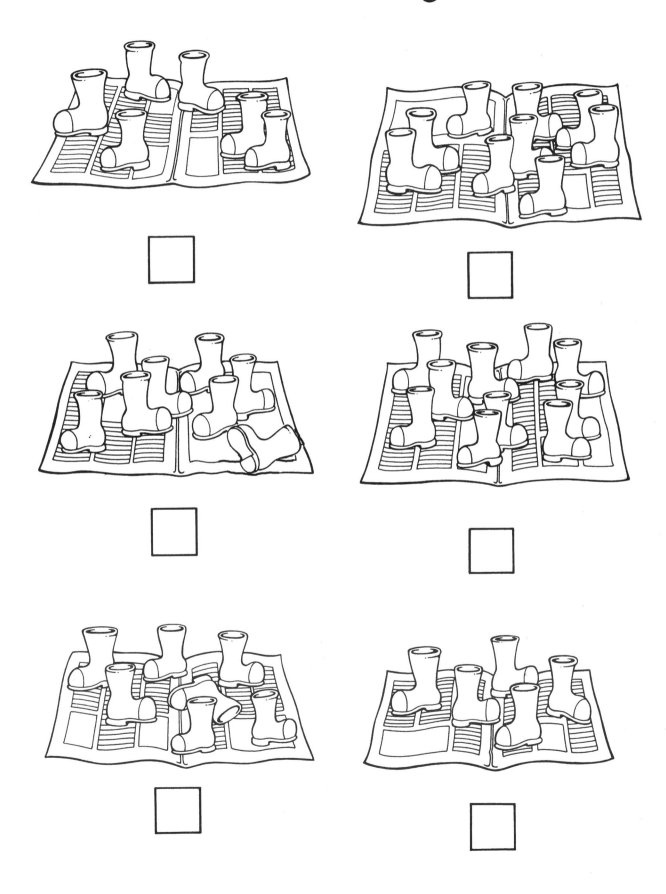

Name _____

How many?

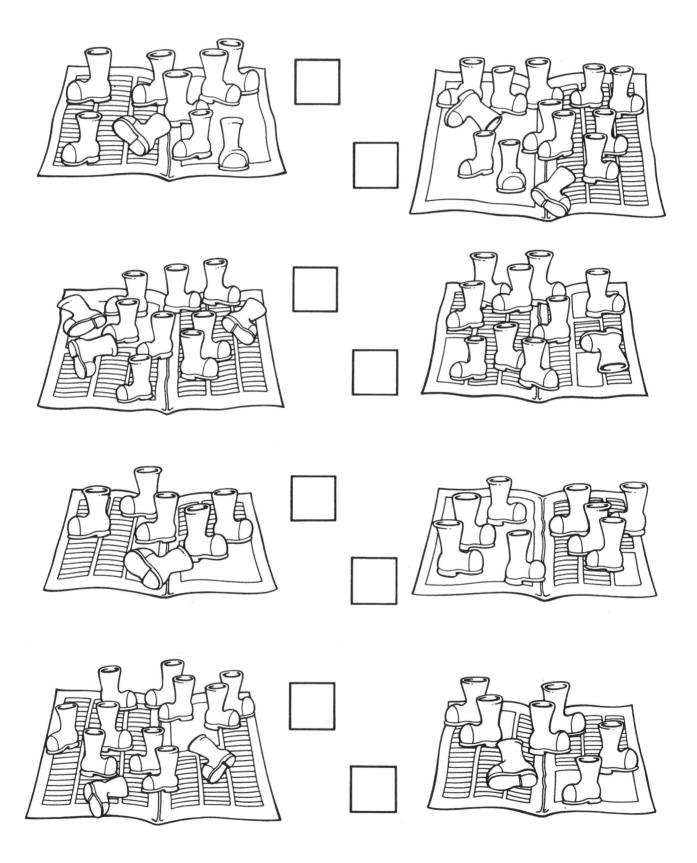

Name _____

Matching

Match the children to the pencils.

 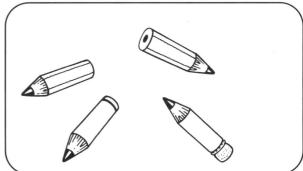

Name _____

Matching

Match the children to the pencils.

Name _____

Matching

Match the children to the pencils.

bigger	biggest
taller	tallest
wider	widest
longer	longest
smaller	smallest
thinner	thinnest
thicker	thickest

Name _____

The biggest thing in our class

The biggest thing in our school

Name _____

Object	Estimate	Real

		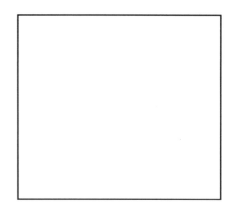

Name _____

On the bus

Name _____

On the bus

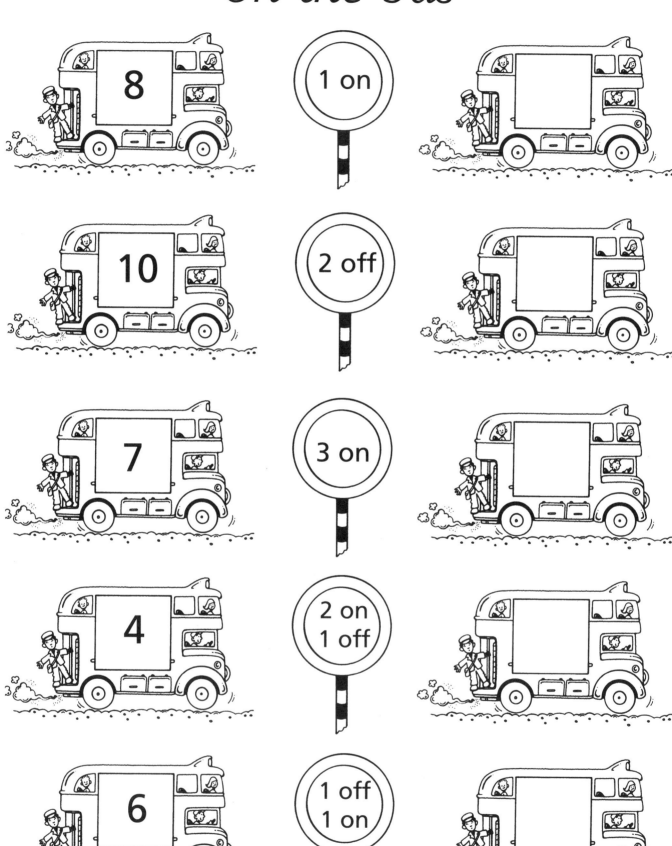

Name _____

On the bus

Name _____

On the bus

Name _____

Make 10!

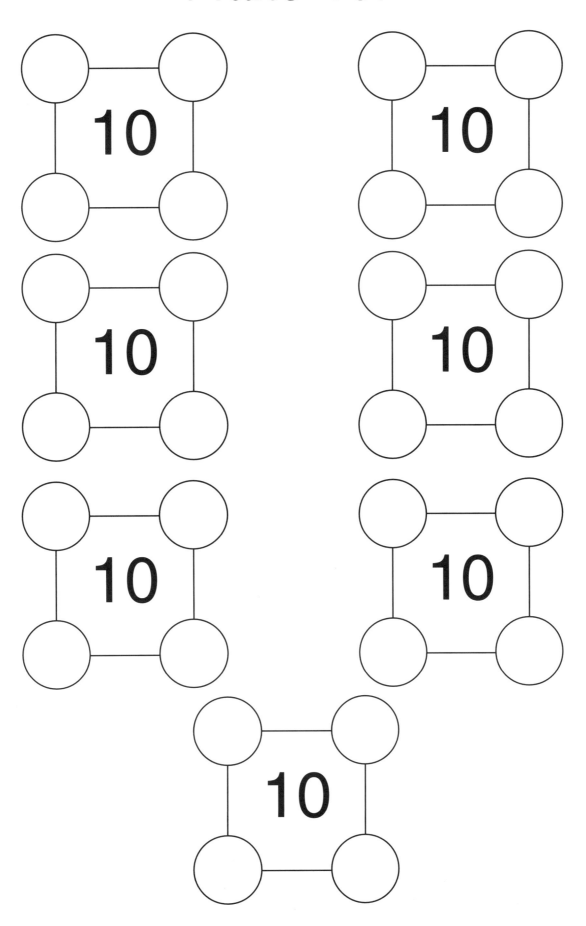

Name _____

What's your target?

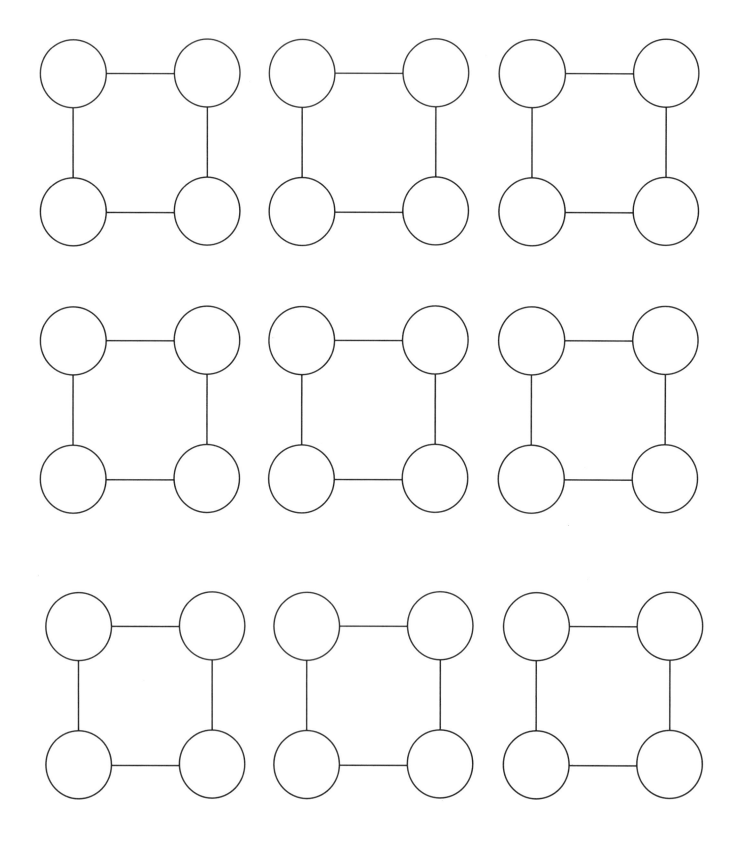

Name _____

How many ways can you make _____ ?

Name _____

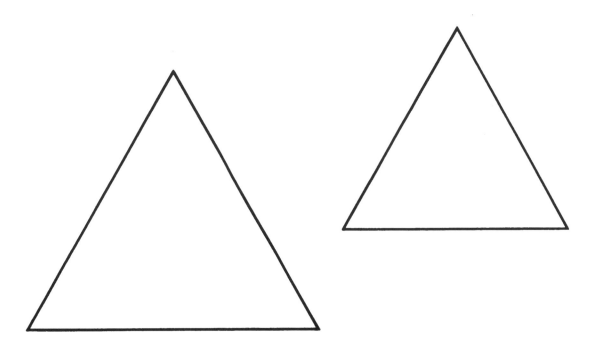

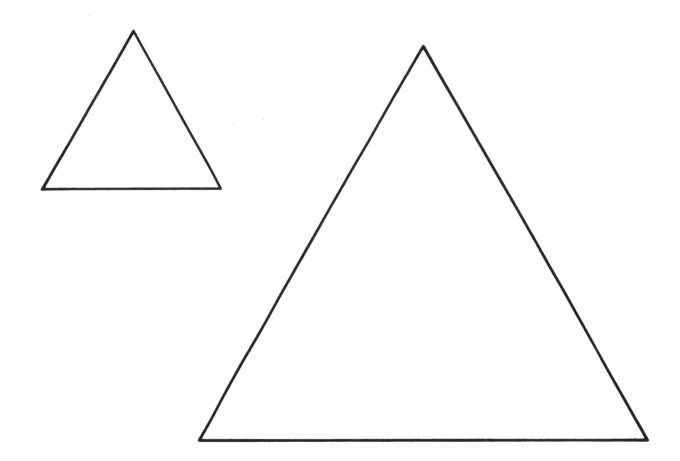

Name _____

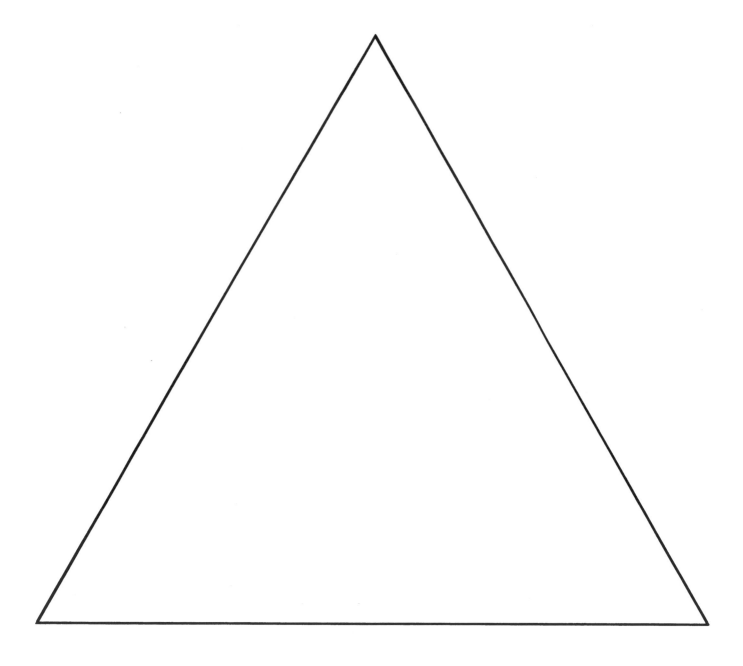

Name _____

Start number	Colour of cube	End number

Colour of cube	Number

Name _____

Apple 9p

Chocolate Twists 29p

Fluff lumps 50p

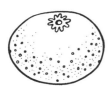

Tangerine 15p

Crisps 35p

Cola drink 72p

Banana 41p

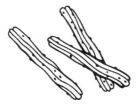

Cheese straws 92p

Orange drink 61p

Peanuts 25p

20 chews 50p

Liquorice 10p

Small packet of biscuits 80p

Sherbet 39p

Name _____

What did you buy?

How much did it cost?

What coins would you use to pay for it?

How much change from a pound would you get?

What did you buy?

How much did it cost?

What coins would you use to pay for it?

How much change from a pound would you get?

Name _____

Estimate how long

1. You can hold your breath for!
   estimate _____ actual _____

2. You can stop blinking!
   estimate _____ actual _____

3. You can say the alphabet without making a mistake!
   estimate _____ actual _____

4. You can stand on one leg!
   estimate _____ actual _____

5. You can balance a book on your head!
   estimate _____ actual _____

6. You can keep your eyes shut!
   estimate _____ actual _____

7. You can balance a ruler on one finger!
   estimate _____ actual _____

8. You can balance a pencil on one finger!
   estimate _____ actual _____

9. You can stare at your partner without laughing!
   estimate _____ actual _____

10. You can be quiet for your teacher!
    estimate _____ actual _____

Name _____

It's about time!

1.   You can hold your breath for!

Difference =

2.   You can stop blinking!

Difference =

3.   You can say the alphabet without making a mistake!

Difference =

4.   You can stand on one leg!

Difference =

5.   You can balance a book on your head!

Difference=

Name _____

It's about time!

6. You can keep your eyes shut!

Difference =

7. You can balance a ruler on one finger!

Difference =

8. You can balance a pencil on one finger!

Difference =

9. You can stare at your partner without laughing!

Difference =

10. You can be quiet for your teacher!

Difference=

January	July
February	August
March	September
April	October
May	November
June	December

Name _____

Name _____

Name _____

100 square

1	2	3	4	5	6	7	8	9	10
11	12	13	14	15	16	17	18	19	20
21	22	23	24	25	26	27	28	29	30
31	32	33	34	35	36	37	38	39	40
41	42	43	44	45	46	47	48	49	50
51	52	53	54	55	56	57	58	59	60
61	62	63	64	65	66	67	68	69	70
71	72	73	74	75	76	77	78	79	80
81	82	83	84	85	86	87	88	89	90
91	92	93	94	95	96	97	98	99	100

Name _____

Odd or even?

4

12

6

10

3

8

11

7

9

1

5

2

Name _____

Odd or even?

21

76

32

65

43

98

87

100

54

7